First published in 2024 by Annalese Press
134 Towngate
Netherthong
Holmfirth
West Yorkshire HD9 3XZ
England

Annalesebooks@gmail.com

Copyright © 2024 Toni Thomas

All rights reserved. No part of this publication may be reproduced, stored, or transmitted in any form, or by any means electronic, mechanical or photocopying, recording or otherwise, without the express written permission of the publisher.

Words and illustrations by Toni Thomas
Book design by Peter Wadsworth

British Library Cataloguing-in-Publication Data
A catalogue record for this book is available on request from the British Library.

ISBN: 978-1-7394457-5-1

Toni Thomas

# In the Mish Mush Universe

With thanks to

rabbits and ferrets and cows and sheep
night hawks and wolves and dolphins that leap
sleepy children awake in the dark
pole beans and mugworts and farmers and carts
parents who bring not just fine cake and pie
but polestar and kisses that light up the sky

## In the mish mush universe

where virtue doesn't need to bark
takes in dewdrop, mud and lark

where sheep meet bog and icicles grow
the day holds more than the things we know

where clouds dance in a barefoot sky
butterflies flirt while passing by

where worms beam their bodies bright
every bed stays snug with light

in the mish mush universe
where shoes sing shanties to the moon
the lake holds feast of fog, swan, loon

where a child like you and me can sup
with beetle foam and buttercup

where starlight holds a dressing gown
that gobbles fear and want and frown

then I will ride my pony wise
show you every version of bold sunrise

take your hand and lead you to
the land of heart that sticks like glue.

## My best friend is a Gumpadore

likes to squeeze in motley door
sip jasmine tea,  prattle much
hold dandelions in his clutch
does not eat big piles of food
is soft and spongy, used to gruel

does not demand a fancy stay
will sleep in clover, layers of hay
knows poems and pranks, wiggly toes
woods where orange nectar grows.

My parents say he's way too big
will crush our roof, our garden, barn
make a mess of what once was farm

but Gumpadores are never cruel
are quick to play the easy fool
like to pause, stand very still
listen hard to stream and hill.

My Gumpadore has fancy skin
sheepish face
never looks out of place.
I take him anywhere I go
to pony shows, the lakes I row
and still he'll be the kind of friend
who always has an ear to lend.

### The Queen can't always have her throne

her kingdom green, her court, her home
sometimes the world turns grey
friends forget her name, won't play
the cakes go limp, are seized by flies
the rain turns thick, there's no sunrise.

The day declines to walk with her
the mist is stiff, the clouds a blur.
Sometimes she must wander sad
search the season some call *glad*.

Queens don't always walk unafraid
upon the pebbly roads we've made
but still the hour reigns down on them
of bud and field, fox, green friend
still quiet things invade the grass
stick around, our moods outlast.

**Bunnies are a funny crew**

worth more than Easter baskets, stew
they hop about woods and field
dig up carrots for their meal
never ask an ounce of me
only that I let them be.

Bunnies are a funny crew
ink up stories, sketches, script
dine on scraps of what we sip
invite April's seeds and sedge
by a mossier tone are fed.

Bunnies recite poems by heart
scatter pellets, onion starts
flirt with daffodils gone frilly
do not mind rocks and hilly.

## Boogle

is big, big, big
bigger than trees
bigger than houses, giraffes, and fleas
bigger than you, bigger than me

is more the conspicuous kind of bard
likes to hide in river, yard
whistle, unearth lost tunes
dine on dandelion root, orchid, loam

will not ask for bed and board
take your dinner table, hoard
trouble you with want and weight
when a forest is on his plate.

No, Boogle is a tender soul
apt to dine on burnt toast
dead bugs, mold
make the little into much
wisk sludge and seaweed
into fudge.

## It's cake in the morning

cake for the noon
cake for the supper
cake for the moon.

A tower of cake
three layers meant to last
sop up the sunlight
drown out the past.

Cake for my lady
cake for my aunt
cake for my brother
cake for the plants

cake for the soup
cake for the room
cake for the cat
who swims with the loon.

Cake for the breakfast
cake for the tea
cake for the bee
cake for me.

So many slices
such a big cake
time to wake early and
*bake, bake, bake!*

### *You are a silly dog* I said

but Bella just shakes her shaggy head
*no, not me, I am the perfect dog for thee.*

Bella likes to race and leap
find the bone in every heap
likes to run with sheep and horse
make our field her own racecourse.

She will not ask for bigger share
make fuss about her tangled hair
will not insist on princely food
on steak and tea
while other folks must dine on pea.

*Bella, Bella come play with me*
and off we go into the grove
where cat meets mouse
and fern and clove
where the river wets our paws
splashes us with fairy lore.

Bella is the dog for me
takes my sodden words and hurt
presses them in finest dirt
when I'm less than I might be
stays loyal friend
a leaping sea.

## Oscar the cat

doesn't always lick our mice
offer up purr and dice
the kind word, cheesy loot
tag games and softest fruit

doesn't always pause to think
a mouse's life isn't only mink
that a parasol alone won't shield
the hunger they can often feel.

No, Oscar isn't always meek
the purry friend with a gentle streak
but when the moon is right
holds certain sway
he'll let them share his rug
his back, his play

yes, when the stars align
Oscar can be very kind
set out plums on a plate
not scold them to *wait, wait, wait*
make a space upon his rug
call them *friend*
not thief or thug.

## Little people

very small, very small
jumping tall, jumping tall
laughing all the way

little people
watch them row, watch them row
come and go, come and go
laughing all the way

little people
slicing cake, slicing cake
muck to rake, muck to rake
laughing all the way

little people
planting dirt, planting dirt
hose to squirt, hose to squirt
laughing all the way

little people
sleepy now, sleepy now
dreaming cows, dreaming cows
sleepy now
snoozing in the hay.

Little people
good to know, good to know
moving slow, moving slow
singing through the day.

## When you see the strange in me

the secret cupboards, unsung sea
do not wince, do not scream
proclaim me as a lizard dream
but keep your faith that strange things hold
a certain magic, certain gold.

When you see the strange in me
the mottled skin, the legs too big
body crooked as a twig
do not wince, do not run
know that strangeness holds great sum
that I can carve fine fruit from ice
concoct poems, tame stubborn mice
make custard out of rancid milk
teach pigs to dance, turn grass to silk

that the world is always slow to see
the miracles of one shy as me.

## To be the Princess

can come with heavy price
beyond the quince and pears
the silk and rice
beyond the field, the trees
everybody asking
*please   please   please*

you try your best to tidy up
skim above a begging cup
make better every forlorn thing
keep the fray of merry May
stapled to your wing all day.

To be a princess is not just
cake and joke and play
the well dries up, the cows want hay
people plead for home and need
the sun gets cross, the mice do scare
the day turns far far from fair.

To be the princess for a day
takes fortitude and weight and stay
a knack for being here
not there
a knowledge of what it means
to care.

## When the snows of January

mawk up your boots
speak of icicled lanes
a thick bubble suit
when you huff puff
your words into the air
till they smoke and steam
then disappear

when the fire in the grate
flames then dims
speaks of ghosts, mud roads
cold cold things

when the cocoa is missing
the streets slight of sled
when your friends are inside
tucked snug in their bed

when the moon wanders out
to see the world white
those puffs of new snow
that launder the night

then don't be afraid
to mount your own star
witness the world as
snow angel, bright bard.

## The bird upon the wing of time

is scarlet and some say half blind
will not steal your finest seed
in the name of extra need
will not in your ear hold screech
when coo words best beseech.

The bird upon the wing of time
does not rush as if the world won't wait
perches easy on rail and gate
waits until the moment's right
to calm your hurts, patch the night

sings a song for me and you
of greenest field and fox and dew.

## These shoes are not thrifty

prone to thin light
they marry the sunshine
blaze through the night.

They take me to places
only sure things can go
to octopus dens
otters that row

they deal with the mud
the snow and the rain
never speak dribble
or constant complain.

These shoes are not thrifty
their tongues never lie
they don't insist polish
or sip dry the sky

they don't ever bargain
over who I must be
cup my toes, my feet
so willingly.

## Though bigness is something

you might dream
like cream on cake, yacht on stream
as if it answers every woe
will cure your doldrums
paint your toes

I'm not sure that big on big
is what we need
won't cause much bother
turn to greed
wonder if squeezing into tiny house
won't crease the floorboards
crush bat and mouse.

Though bigness has its virtues bright
it sometimes can lack true insight
doesn't seem to measure much
or sup with stars, be discreet
when modest often washes feet.

So what we wish for and what we get
must make a rope without regret
take the gnat, the fly, the birds
act not the empire that only herds
allow space for bud and bee
bend down low, let others see.

## Raccoon

I don't have an easy life
avoiding roadways, fields of ice

sometimes no one cares to see
my sleek coat, well-shaped paws
the clever way I sidestep cars.

They do not know my trials and woe
the shrunken woods where I must go
how some things whittle me
when food is scarce
nothing's free.

It can be a lonely life
staying shy of hunt and strife
moving on with scant to eat
keeping time by my own heartbeat

but the snow still asks to marry me
the stars across the sky don't flee
the sun never long runs away
returns to light a brand new day.

### Lion, Lion

bright am I
a beam of flame
while clouds drift by

an elegant body
built for speed and length
the miles and miles I must commence.

Lion, Lion
bright am I
fierce looking in the small man's sky
but noble still for those who see
the miracle that remains quite me.

**Please bestow**

a dram of milk, wild wet kiss
way to show your inborn bliss
don't be shy, run away
when elfish beings come to stay.

We who travel far and near
bring our bells, our pointy shoes
our songs that wash away your blues

we who bring cake and cream
ducks and pigs that twirl and dream
bring our stories of sod and sea
hedgehog and royal bee.

Please bestow an ounce of mirth
when you see what we can birth.

### The paper horn

I blow and honk
was once in a prince's trunk
holds embroidered thread
likes to climb and crown my head.
This horn has known a past of thieves
of scallywags and ships and deeds.

My paper horn is very fine
of purple hope and want and twine
of riotous star and milky cream
all the things that go unseen.

Like the goose upon the lake
I *honk honk honk*
welcome each daybreak.

## Blind William

isn't a mouse to mind
he's very smart and quite quite kind
will offer brew and bell and whistle
lead you out of bog and thistle

will not see the muck of you
the clumped dirt
the stench, the glue
will not insist you marry him
pack your bags
divorce your kin.

No, Blind William's not a mouse to fear
his words hold cream
his eyes a stair
he'll rescue birds
make ginger stew
mint new words just for you

offer up a scouting map
that holds marbled eggs
in a velvet sack.

## In the riff ruff course of day

when piddle monsters come out to play
wreck the yard, scare the birds
slice the lawn in halves and thirds

when they steal your glass of milk
your chalk, your dog, your cake, your silk
drive the sun so far away

do not say what they want to hear
*life's not easy, runs on fear*
just let them fume and huff and puff
blow off steam
then wash them in love's better stream.

### The hedgehog who stole the bread

wasn't sorry to be fed
didn't thank the baker, pet the cat
just said *I will be back.*

This creature who some called *greedy*
didn't have a friend or theory
sloffed the mold off oat and rye
took the leftovers we don't prize.

The hedgehog who stole the bread
*wasn't thinking right* you said
which is true, but sometimes
hunger consumes a yard
erases sight of dandelion and bard.

## Carousel

Forward and back
we sometimes go
one minute tattered
the next finely sewed

the sky burnt all amber
the clouds slipped away
the birds watching close
to see how we play

the dark only tickling
the night sky a hymn
the daylight a cooking
our cups to the brim.

Forward and backward
then round and round
our horses ungainly
as we lift off the ground.

## When your words are five parts

whimper, two parts woe
dig about
no place to go

when the hours are thin
the milkman's gone
the cock won't crow
the fairy slip's torn

then take a lesson straight from me
it's time to find a different story

build a boat that's compact, tough
can ride amid the debris, the duff
make it nimble, make it sweet
a cup for all your dreams to keep

bring along a snack or two
a roll, an apple
your heart's firm glue.

### *Be mine* the day said

but I was not ready
was filled with wants
and quite quite heady.

*Be mine* the night said
but I couldn't listen
amid my toys and bears
stuffed kittens.

*Be mine* the slow child said at school
but I was little and still a fool
so I ran away to play
with others who gobbled the day.

*Be mine* the sky said
while I sighed
and she offered me up a lullaby.

*Be mine* the sun said as I prayed
for more gifts to be laid.

*Be mine* the moon whispered
as I slept
while up above the stars wept.

*Be mine Be mine Be mine*
was shouted all day in my ear
while the sheep stood still in the field
for they could already hear.

**My mother says the goat I keep**

cheats us out of milk and sleep
is far too noisy, not a friend
will demolish what we lend.

My goat is not the kind to pause
be slow to move, indulge the stars
likes to make her presence known
dine on delicacies
dust her throne.

My goat never refuses to see
the majesty that is she.

## If an antelope comes to town

she'll lap up fountains
parkland, crown
talk savanna, sunset gold
splash on paints, tales of old
stay up late inventing news
never mire in others shoes.

If an antelope comes to town
and everyone is fast asleep
into our kitchen she'll silent creep
brew up cups of milky tea
pancake batter for you and me
grill each one the way we like
with blueberry lumps, sugar spikes.

The pancakes will rise and rise
in piles so high they reach the sky.
You've never known a treat
until pancakes tall as a city
with an antelope you eat.

## Better days are about to come

I feel them in my pinky finger
know they're here to bless and linger
with willow tree and grassy bed
silly scarf to dress my head
a brand new bud, open door
furry friend soon in store.

Special things are on the way
for those of us who dream and play
who out of mud can make an ark
find bread in dirt and licks in bark.

So do not fear the silent night
a starless sky scrubbed less bright
do not wish for just pretty things
a brand new bike, toy that rings

when you can trust
that what's inside
is gold endowed
remains quite enough.

### The day will not let go of me

talks of boats, a sailing sea
talks of orange fish and tides
maypole dances, kites that fly.

The night speaks circles
but the day speaks cake
and all the stories meadows make

speaks to me of spotted dog
emerald grass and imp and bog

speaks to me of silly things
clothespin dolls and purple wings.

### The journey of tadpole

is often not seen
is part wonder, good earth
the promise of dream.

It happens in April
while some of us sleep
while tulips and crocus
first flies start to leap.

The journey of tadpole
is no easy thing
means transforming
from one to another
come spring.

Some of us hanker
for this same kind of birth
to magically rise
from sadness to mirth.

## Rhinoceros are hard to handle

eat you out of house and plate
refuse to don clean napkin
sit and wait.

They like to bask in fiercest sun
roll in mud, call it fun
never let me ride on them
comb their coat
invite a friend.

I've seldom met
such a stubborn lot
intent to wallow
in mucky spot.

They sing the jungle
sing the grass
concoct mud stew of their past
hold a faith
the earth, the brownish stream
will keep them clean.

## The angel you once did know

may not be the one who comes in snow.
Some things dim and some things flame
angels like people can do the same.

So when at night you care to dream
of places far, sights unseen
make room for the one who comes
with bell and sled
silly buds about her head

do not fear, turn away
but answer clear – *please come to stay*
because certain angels will see us through
the darkest hour and cling like glue.

## The Fizzywicks

I'm off to where the Fizzywicks live
with my wee sack and walking boots
place of wood and grouse and coots.

In case the dark turns very thick
and wolves sound their loud alarm
I'll have my wits, my bread, my wick
the Fizzywicks to keep me warm.

Up the valley where the Fizzywicks live
I'm off to have a fine old time
place where odd kingdom
meets fish and rhyme
where the river runs wild
for child and beast
and every day's a Fizzywick feast.

## I like you like this

just the way you are
a half sung landscape
brightness of star

like your pasture
your cows, pigs, and sheep
the way they can lounge
free in your keep

like the way your eyes
echo the sea
cause dolphins to jump
no angels to flee

like how your words
are porous and wise
mothered by clouds
an unseen sunrise

like how you counsel
keep pace with the moon
rename dark creatures
always leave room

like how you plant in me
such mysterious things
pocket lost flowers
the gifts the rain brings.

## Make no mistake

this world is for you
made of twig and iris, fern, modest glue
comes on a wind, feathers the day
has no special wrapping
no wants to display

will ask nothing of you
insist that you mind
find only kindness
when the day also holds brine.

Make no mistake
this world is for you
ribboned with creatures
so varied and rich
their coats are a medley
of the earth's holy pitch

they come not for money
come not out of greed
come to spread joy
good offerings, seed

won't demand ransom
for what they can give
just smudge you in scent
show how to live.

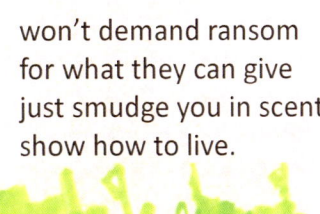

Toni lives in a hobbit size house in Oregon where she likes to write poems and whip up mango ice cream. At night her dog Bella dreams mud baths and treats from the dolls. One day they hope to travel in a gypsy caravan surrounded by birds.

She has published nineteen poetry collections, appeared in over fifty literary magazines and won several awards. This is her fifth children's book.

www.ingramcontent.com/pod-product-compliance
Lightning Source LLC
Chambersburg PA
CBRC091725070526
44585CB00009B/174